This book is dedicated to the Saskatoon Public Library Young Adult Department: Rena, Laureen and Diane.

BG

Chapter One

THE WHOLE THING started right after I erased my left eyebrow. Not that I'd meant to. Tuesday night I'd gone into high gear plucking my eyebrows. The next day I looked like I'd leaned too close to a Bunsen burner during a science experiment. This is big-time trauma when you're fifteen. I had to go around trying to keep my missing eyebrow covered with my left hand. That was the day Brent Floyd decided to ask me to the Valentine's Day dance.

There I was at my locker, dumping my books. I was on my way to the Camera Club to develop a series of shots I'd taken around home. Mom and I share a house with my friend Sophie and her mother. I had taken some funny shots of Sophie and my dog Popcorn.

"Hey, Jujube!"

For as long as I can remember, everyone's called me Jujube. It's because I have one blue eye and one green eye. And now — one eyebrow. I looked up to see Brent coming down the hall. Of course, my brain stopped working. It always does in a crisis. I'd only liked the guy for about a decade — not that I admitted it to anyone. And it's tough trying to look casual with your left hand glued to your forehead.

"Hi, Brent."

Brent leaned against the next locker

and looked at my lips. Whenever Brent talks to a girl, he looks at her lips. The hand on my forehead was getting sweaty.

"I suppose a hundred different guys have asked you out for this Friday?" he asked my lips.

When Brent's nervous, he starts joking around. His being nervous made me nervous. My mind went blank. "Friday?"

"Yeah. Y'know — Friday? This is Wednesday. Then there's Thursday and then Friday. The dance, remember?" he teased.

"Oh yeah — the dance." My hand slipped and I got it back up into place.

He leaned closer. "Want to go with me?"

The guy who had his locker next to me came up behind Brent and said, "Excuse me," very loudly. I wanted to knock him one good one with my geography textbook.

"Sure," I said quickly before Brent moved — and changed his mind.

"Great!" he grinned, still looking at my lips.

Friday evening, Brent had to be at the school early to help the band set up. He didn't pick me up until 7:30. Sophie had to check out "the latest," and Mom put him through Twenty Questions at the door. She's pretty military with my boyfriends.

"Whew! I wasn't sure we'd get out alive," Brent said as we walked to his car.

I grinned. "It's called motherly love. Don't leave home without it."

I'd gotten used to having one eyebrow and had stopped living with a hand attached to my forehead. First dates usually give me lockjaw, but Brent's joking around helped. When we got to the dance, the two of us were having a great time. There was the usual problem with the slower numbers — figuring out whose hands go where, that sort of thing.

Brent liked to dance really close, closer than I was used to. Half of me wondered if we'd leave body imprints on each other. The other half wanted to start taking his shirt off.

Partway through the dance, Brent had to go talk to the band about something. I wandered over to talk to Carlos, this guy I'd gotten to know in the Camera Club. He's the loner type and doesn't talk much. He was in his jean jacket as usual, leaning against a back wall. I leaned up next to him and watched Brent talk to the drummer.

"So you're here with Mr. Warp Speed." Carlos took a drink from his Coke.

"Mr. Warp Speed?" I asked.

Carlos looked at me for a moment, then grinned and handed me his Coke. "Brent."

I drank, trying to cover the blush I felt taking over my face. "Hey, two hours and I'm still a virgin."

Carlos laughed.

"And proud of it," we chanted together. Guys and girls get the same message in our sex ed classes.

"So who're you here with?" I hadn't noticed him with anyone and I wanted to get him back for Brent's nickname.

Carlos shrugged. "Just came to hear the band."

"Yeah, right. Whoever she is, you're probably too scared to call her up," I teased.

"Maybe." Carlos looked away.

Brent came up to us then. "Jujube — I've got to get something for the band from my car. Come with me to get it?"

Carlos watched us leave without a word. Sometimes deep dark moods drop down on him like the dead of night. Then it's like talking to someone in a coma. At the door, I turned and waved to him. He was still watching us.

Outside, Brent took my hand and we ran through the February cold. It was minus ten — not bad if you're wearing a jacket. Brent shivered as he unlocked the car door.

"Quick — get in. No, not the front, the back," he said.

I dove into the back seat, thinking this must be where the band equipment was. Brent crawled in after me, then pulled the car door closed.

"God, it's cold." He leaned over the front seat and started the car. Then he dropped back and pulled me in against him. Suddenly, I was warm all over. In the dark, close to him like that, it was easy for things to happen. His mouth went soft as I brushed mine back and forth across it. I put my hand on his throat and felt the way his low moans moved under my fingers.

"I lied," he whispered.

"What?" The school, the dance, the other kids had faded away.

Brent laughed into my ear. "I didn't have to get anything. I just wanted a chance to talk to you."

"About what?" Suddenly, I heard Carlos in my head. *Mr. Warp Speed*, I thought.

"This," Brent said, kissing my throat. He started to fiddle with the top button of my shirt. "Let me make this very clear," he added.

As soon as we'd started kissing, I'd known Brent didn't have to get anything for the band. It hadn't mattered — I wasn't about to check out of a dream come true. But now, there was something about his tone and laugh that bothered me. It was as if Brent thought he'd pulled one over on me — as if I was some beginner he had to explain things to.

"Hey, just a sec," I said, pulling back

a little. The good feeling was sliding away. We felt like two very separate bodies in the back of a very cold car again. I started thinking about carbon monoxide poisoning. I was too young to die . . . for love or sex.

"C'mon, Jujube. I've really liked you for a long time now," Brent said.

"Yeah, me too." But I was tucking in my shirt. I wanted to think. There was a bad feeling crawling around my stomach that wouldn't go away.

"So, no prob — right?" He tried to kiss me again. The feeling in my stomach grew.

"No!"

"What are you afraid of ?"

"I'm not afraid." And I wasn't. There was something I knew I wanted to think about, but I couldn't get at it.

"Girls are always a bit afraid of this," he said.

How would you know? Have you

ever been a girl? I thought. My voice came out differently than I wanted it to — angry.

"I'm not into diving into things at warp speed, Brent. Let's go back in, O.K.?" I said.

Chapter Two

Before I knew it, Carlos's nickname had come out of my mouth. Brent stared at me like he'd been hit hard.

"What'd you say? Warp speed?" He sounded as if it hurt him to speak.

I realized he'd heard that nickname before — a lot. "Nothing. It's just, like, we don't have to do everything tonight, right?"

That wasn't what I'd meant to say.

I'd liked what we were doing just as much as he had. But words were coming out of my mouth weirdly and I couldn't figure out how to fix them. It was just that everything suddenly felt wrong.

Brent stared off, his face angry in the dim light coming from the streetlights. When he turned back, the anger was wiped away, his face friendly like always.

"We've hardly done everything," he said.

I flushed. Now I felt stupid.

He leaned back and was quiet for a moment. "Man, you can really make me feel good," he said softly.

"Really?"

"Yeah."

We talked for a bit, then he cut the motor and we walked back to the gym. Just inside the door, he leaned over and we kissed.

"Sorry," he said.

I could see kids watching us. I was

so relieved that things were O.K. between us again that I grinned at them. When I looked up at Brent, I saw him grinning too. The rest of the night went like that — one big grin. When Brent dropped me off at my house, we sat there looking at each other's lips. I reached over and touched his mouth.

"I like you," I said.

"A lot?" he murmured against my fingers.

"A lot. See you Monday."

I watched his car drive off into the falling snow. I decided to forget that bad moment in the back seat as if it'd never happened.

I spent the weekend studying for tests and reading *The Taming of the Shrew* for English. Old Dead Lips, our teacher, was a major problem if you didn't get your work done.

Sophie, my roommate, studies in front of the TV with a textbook open in her lap in case someone walks in. Sophie's three years older than me. A few years back, her parents split up because her father was beating Sophie up. He went to jail for six months. Sophie had to live in a group home while her mother went into an alcohol rehab program. It was a rough year and she ended up flunking grade ten. After the rehab program, Sophie and her mother moved in with us.

"How's your chem coming along?" I asked her.

Sophie was watching Saturday morning cartoons. She asked, "How was your date? Any good chemistry there?"

Sophie likes to tease me about sex. Her boyfriend is away at college so all she can do is talk about it.

"It was O.K." I knew I was going red.

Sophie laughed. "Learn anything new?"

I groaned. She was really missing her boyfriend. "Brent's got a nickname — 'Mr. Warp Speed.'"

Sophie frowned. "Is he like that?"

I shrugged.

Sophie grinned. "If he was, you'd know by now."

Brent didn't call all weekend. I wondered about that, but not a lot. After all, I didn't call him either. I was still looking forward to first period, Monday morning — English. As I walked through the doorway, I could hear Brent's voice, the kids around him laughing.

Always the joker, I thought.

I turned toward him and there he was, leaned back in his desk like always. He was looking right at me. I started to smile. Then I noticed all the kids around him were looking at me too. I glanced away from them, back to Brent. For a second, he looked like he was in some sort of fast pain. Then a grin came up on his face and it was gone.

"Hi," I made myself say.

It wasn't Brent who answered. The guy next to him grinned and said, "Jujube — bet you feel like some new woman, eh?"

The group started to laugh. I opened my mouth to say something back, anything, but no words came. Brent wasn't looking at me anymore. Instead, he had his head down, grinning sideways at the guy who'd spoken. Someone punched his shoulder.

Then Brent leaned across the aisle and started talking to another girl. Everyone turned away from me as if I wasn't there anymore. *Something* had just happened. But I couldn't figure out what it was. *Or could I?* Either way, I couldn't keep standing around as if time had stopped. My chin came up and carried me over to my seat behind Carlos. I dropped myself and my textbooks into my desk like a two-ton truck.

"Hey," Carlos said. He was turned around in his desk.

"What?" I stared out the window. I needed a couple of minutes to figure things out.

Carlos tugged at one of my fingers. "Hey."

I had to look at him.

"They're jerks," he said. He hung onto my hand as if it was some sort of prize.

Suddenly, I was blinking fast. "Yeah?"

"Yeah."

Old Dead Lips stood up and cleared his throat. Then he asked someone to give him the plot of *The Taming of the Shrew*. As usual, all he got was the sound of a lot of breathing. Then one of the guys over by Brent spoke up.

"It's about this guy who wants to get this girl. She plays hard to get but really she's pretty easy. She gives in. They get married. The end."

"You make it sound like a Friday night movie," Old Dead Lips said.

"Same old story," the guy shrugged. Some of the kids around him laughed.

Everything in me stopped — everything. Even the snow falling outside seemed to jerk to a halt halfway between sky and ground. I wanted everything to stay stopped like that. Then I wouldn't have to know what came next. What my gut was telling me.

Ahead of me, Carlos shifted in his seat, then spoke up. Surprise got my brain going again — Carlos never talked in class. "I dunno, maybe I just don't get it," he said.

"What don't you understand?" Old Dead Lips asked.

Carlos flicked his pen against his

desktop. I watched his ears go dark red. "Why'd she marry the guy? He seems like a real jerk to me."

For the first time that term, Old Dead Lips came alive. His eyebrows went up and his mouth dropped open. I thought, *Uh-oh, Carlos is going to flunk this course for sure.*

"Well, Carlos, I guess that means you've actually read the play," he said.

Carlos's ears turned purple. First time he'd spoken up in class and Old Dead Lips was putting him down for it. I put up my hand.

"Yes, Trudy?"

That's my real name. "I'm with Carlos. I think the guy's a real jerk, too."

Old Dead Lips gave me a look that put me in deep freeze. "Anyone else in the class agree with these two?"

No one said a word. This seemed to cheer Old Dead Lips up. "Everyone turn to Act I."

I poked Carlos in the back and whispered, "Thanks."

He shifted sideways in his seat and smiled. "Old Dead Lips is a jerk, too."

Chapter Three

I had this feeling — like the *Titanic* had sunk inside my stomach. It wouldn't go away. Carlo's being nice couldn't change that. But I had a test about land forms in my next class to think about. Staring down at the test paper, I wanted to write: Basic rock form — Brent Floyd. But I didn't. It looked like I might've flunked my social life. But I wanted to pass geography.

21

Besides, I still liked Brent — a lot. I figured it was all a mistake. I'd talk to him and we'd clear everything up. I was walking down an aisle in the cafeteria at lunch when it started again.

"Hey, Jujube!"

They were sitting right on the aisle, leaning out toward me — a bunch of Brent's friends. Well, they were my friends too. Sometimes I ate lunch with them. I smiled. None of these guys was in my English class.

"Hi, guys."

Someone gave a low whistle.

"Hi, Jujube," someone replied, but his voice was different, as if we shared a secret. What secret? They were all grinning.

I wasn't going to let the same thing happen again. Eyes narrowed, I shifted into a very careful position. I tried to look a little bored. "What's so funny?"

"What's so funny?" a guy named

Ralph repeated. Last week, he'd beaten me at poker. "I dunno. You tell us."

Something cold and wet ran down my hand. My Canada Dry was spilling.

"Back seat baby," Ralph said, sort of singsong. The guys snickered.

Something in me went into a long fall. Around me, kids kept shouting and laughing. A teacher walked by. To everyone else, we probably looked like friends talking.

We are friends talking, I thought.

I set my pop and French fries on the table. "You're kidding, right?"

Ralph looked away from me to another guy. "What do you think, Scott — a seven?"

Scott looked me up and down. "Seven? Maybe."

"Maybe on a good day," said another guy.

"A really good day? Like last Friday?" Ralph replied.

They were all laughing again.

"You guys are pigs," I said.

They shut up for a moment. Then Ralph muttered something. Probably I should've left it and walked off. But I was so mad.

"What'd you say, Ralph?" I asked.

He sort of grinned but kept quiet and wouldn't look at me. I walked around the table so I was opposite him. "Pass that math test I helped you study for, Ralph?" I asked.

Ralph poked at his sandwich. I could see a slow red coming up his neck. Still not looking at me, he said, "Ah, forget it, Jujube."

"Yeah, right." I started to walk back to pick up my food when Scott spoke up. He said it loud and clear, so everyone could hear.

"He said you were a ten at the dance, Jujube. No — in the parking lot. A perfect score. A real pro."

It was like they'd run me at top speed into a concrete wall. For a moment, there was nothing. Then a hand touched my elbow.

"C'mon," Carlos said into my ear.

"Oh, now Carlos gets lucky," Scott said.

Carlos stopped. He turned and stared at them. Their eyes dropped.

Carlos can do this, I thought. *He's a guy.*

"Hey, Scott — you going to band practice after school?" someone finally said to change the subject.

Carlos and I walked out of the cafeteria. When we found an empty stairway, we sat down.

"You all right?" Carlos ate my French fries. I stared off, not talking. I couldn't seem to find my voice.

"Jujube?"

I whispered, "They've never talked like that before."

"Sure they have," Carlos said.

"Not to me."

"O.K., so not to you."

I knew what he was saying. I'd even laughed sometimes, when they put another girl down. I guess I'd just never thought it could happen to me.

"I thought they were my friends."

"Some friends."

"They'll burn me."

"Maybe." He just sat there, chewing on a French fry.

Like, my life is ending here, I thought.

"I didn't do . . .what they're saying," I said.

Carlos snorted. "I'm not your mother. It's nobody's business what you did."

"Yeah, I know, but it's worse when it's all lies."

Carlos shrugged. "Some guys lie about that stuff all the time. They think if they don't score, they're a nobody. So they lie."

"You're a guy," I pointed out.

He grinned at me. "Yeah?"

"So do you lie about it?"

"I tell them it's none of their business."

I watched him drink my pop. "What else are they saying about me?"

"You really want to know?"

"May as well."

Carlos looked pretty tense. "I'll keep it as polite as I can. They're saying you're easy, you're fast. You'll go all the way on the first date. You'll do anything a guy wants. I won't go into the details."

I wanted to disappear. Kids in that cafeteria were passing my name around like a dirty joke. I'd seen other girls this had happened to. They waited for everyone to get tired of the rumors and wear the jokes out. Sometimes the stories died down. Sometimes they didn't. I couldn't stick around for that.

I took the half-empty container of

pop, and threw it hard against the wall. Then I stood there swearing for a long time. Carlos sat and waited me out. When I was finished, he looked impressed.

"They're scum, Jujube," he said.

I half-laughed. I wanted to cry. "Rumors run this school. It doesn't matter who starts them."

"So let them talk," Carlos said.

He wasn't quite getting it. "Carlos, there are about two thousand kids in this school, right? So, say each one of them makes one joke about me — that's two thousand jokes I have to put up with. Even if I don't hear them, they're out there. I'll feel them. And what if they just laugh? Say each one laughs, 'Ha ha ha!' That makes six thousand 'Ha's' I have to live through."

Carlos sighed. "Look, you can let scum run you or you can let them run each other. Just walk back in there now like you're the truth and they're the lies."

I tried. Carlos and I went into the cafeteria and walked through the crowd of voices to the other end. It felt a little like a parade, everyone secretly watching me. A couple of kids said, "Hi." No one yelled a word about my sex life. But it was what they were thinking — I could feel the vibes coming at me two thousand strong.

Chapter Four

That afternoon felt unreal. Everything looked the same but felt different. Running laps around the gym, I'd forget what had happened. Then the feeling would come back. *Something's wrong*, I'd think, looking around me. *Things look normal, but something's weird. What's wrong with this picture?*

Then I'd find the answer somewhere

around my stomach. *It was me.* Even if Brent was the one spreading those lies, he was making me wear them. Unreal — the whole thing felt so unreal.

So when I turned on "Star Trek" after school, I felt at home. Floating in outer space, away from all this — that's what I wanted. Popcorn laid his head on my feet with a sigh. His first owners were from Scotland. Whenever Scotty came on, yelling to Captain Kirk, Popcorn thumped his tail.

To go where no man has gone before, I thought. *To go where the stars first send out their light.*

"I can't help it, Captain — these engines are about to blow!" yelled the TV Scotty. Popcorn wagged his tail.

At supper, Sophie was upset. Now that her father was off probation, he was allowed to call her mom again. He didn't call her at our house because Sophie, Mom, and I hung up on him. He called her at work, and tonight she'd gone out for dinner with him. Sophie kept stabbing her mashed potatoes. Globs ended up on the table. But Mom didn't complain.

"Why does she talk to him? What if she moves back with him?" Sophie demanded.

Mom sighed, "I don't know, Sophie."

"But he went to jail for hurting us," Sophie said.

In a way, I was glad Mom had Sophie to worry about. Every now and then she'd give me one of her long thinking looks. What this usually means is a talk about condoms and the meaning of life. This is part of being an only child. Mom has major panic attacks when I come down with a cold. But, like I said, she can get pretty military — she works as a meatpacker at Gainers. I knew if I told her about Brent, she'd flip out and go after the entire school.

Fortunately, Mom had to head off for her evening shift without a chance to come after me. She stood in the doorway, zipping up her parka. "Jujube?"

"Yeah?"

"Don't think I don't know something's bothering you." Mom's eyes are traffic-light green.

"Oh, Mom — I'm all right. Have fun shoving raw meat around." I kissed her goodbye and went up to the bedroom I share with Sophie. Popcorn and I flopped down on my bed. Sophie sat on hers, staring out the cold, black window. Stars were out, shining like faraway friends.

"I know you're upset, but can I tell you something?" I asked.

Sophie's eyes were red. "That's why you only ate carrots at supper?"

"Maybe."

Sophie pulled a bag of Oreos out of

the night table between our beds. "Here, eat this junk. You must be hungry."

I munched out on Oreos and told her what had happened with Brent. Sophie sat listening and stroking a stuffed mouse she'd had since she was a kid. Finally she said, "Remember when I first went into the group home? Well, it got around school pretty fast. Someone started a rumor that I was doing time for hooking."

"What?" I'd never heard about this.

"I didn't tell anyone. It was really bad — everyone telling jokes, bugging me. One time they even wrote things on the blackboard."

"Who started it?"

Sophie gave a small laugh. "It doesn't matter who starts it. It's weird; the way kids gang up on someone. It's like they only feel strong when they're in a group, putting someone else down."

"But I haven't done anything to them."

Sophie hugged her worn-out mouse.

"It's a power rush sort of thing. A good rep, a bad rep — a rep is something other people give you. They know they can turn you into anything they want — that's the rush."

I thought about it. "So what finally happened?"

"After a while they found someone else to bug and forgot about me."

We heard the front door open. It was Sophie's mother coming in. Sophie jumped out of bed and ran down the hall. As I listened to their voices, I picked up Sophie's beat-up mouse. Popcorn whined. Maybe Sophie had made it through O.K., but I knew they'd hurt her. It made me mad.

Over the next few days, things died down at school — just a few comments here and there. But the rumors were still going around and showing up in strange places. Like the moment Carlos and I came out of the darkroom together. The other kids in the Camera Club started to grin and snort. They wouldn't have done that before. Of course, not all of the kids behaved that way. Some went out of their way to be friendly, act like nothing was going on. And it wasn't like all my old friends dropped me or anything. It was just that if a comment about me came up, they'd laugh. *Even the girls*. I tried hard to turn the whole thing into a joke and laugh along with them.

At least I didn't have to see much of Brent. I used to bump into him all over the place. Not anymore. It was like I was some germ he was avoiding. But we were still stuck in the same room in English class. There, he sat with his friends across the room and laughed at their jokes, never even looking at me. After about a week of this, I was passed a note. Old Dead Lips was writing on the board. The note was folded up small, my name written across the front.

Slowly, it spread apart in my hand.

All over the page, someone had drawn pictures of couples having sex. Under each girl was written my name. Each guy got a different name. *"Getting into the family business"* was written across the top. *Sophie*, I thought, as the meaning hit home. Everyone knew Sophie lived with me. Everyone thought of us as sisters.

"Let me see it." Carlos had his hand stretched out toward me. I shook my head and stared out the window.

"C'mon," he insisted.

"Carlos, perhaps you could tell us ..." Old Dead Lips was on Carlos's case again. Relieved, I stuck the note into *The Taming of the Shrew*. After class, I took off. I was halfway down the hall when Carlos caught up.

"Let me see it." He had one hand on my arm.

"No." I tried to pull away. But he

37

reached out and took my book. As he read the note, Carlos talked under his breath in fast Spanish. I stared at a nearby fire safety poster.

"You're letting them tell you who you are," he said.

I wanted to shove him so hard he'd join Spock in outer space. "No, I'm not."

"Yes, you are."

I yelled at him. "This is not happening to you. This is happening to me. So don't tell me what I think. And don't tell me how to feel."

He didn't turn and walk away like I expected. He looked at me and said, "Sorry."

My next words came out of the place that hurt the most. "It feels like it's true, Carlos. Once they say it, that's the way it feels. I *know* it's not, but it *feels* like if everyone's saying it, somehow it must be true."

"I'm not saying it," he reminded me. "You're hardly everyone."

He was quiet, watching me. Maybe now he was finally starting to get it. "It hurts, Carlos. It hurts like hell."

I took the note out of his hand. As I shoved it back into my book, Sophie walked up.

Perfect timing, I thought. Since she was in grade twelve, I hardly ever saw her.

"What's the matter?" she asked.

"Nothing."

"You look like the end of the world," she said.

Carlos glared at me. I handed Sophie the note. *Getting into the family business.* I watched her read it.

Sophie doesn't swear much. When she does, I learn new ways words can be put together. Carlos got that impressed look again.

"Family business, huh?" Sophie tore up the note and threw it into a nearby garbage pail. Then she put an arm around me. "We'll show them family."

Chapter Five

After the note, things kept up, steady as a heartbeat. Most of it didn't seem to have much to do with Brent anymore. He probably didn't even know about a lot of it. Still, I blamed him. Just thinking about him made my hands go to fists. He'd started all this. Now, guys I didn't know and had never talked to made comments in the hall.

"Busy Friday?" someone would call out.

"Busy at lunch?" another would add.

They never actually touched me, but it felt like they had — wherever they wanted. I kept trying to smile, treat it like a joke. I'd say, "Real busy," and walk away. I told myself there were other things to think about. Old Dead Lips had given the class a project called "Ways We Communicate — TV, Movies, Radio, Books." I tried to focus on this since it was due in a couple of weeks.

Things were heating up between Sophie and her mother. I got home one afternoon to hear Sophie arguing on the phone. "But you promised we'd go to a movie this weekend, Mom!"

The phone slammed down. When I came into the kitchen, Sophie was tearing open a package of graham crackers. When she's upset, Sophie eats. Then she complains that she's fat.

I picked up the graham crackers.

"You can have three. That's it." I started to walk out with the package.

Sophie's voice was thin, as if stretched over a terrible sadness. "Mom's spending the weekend at Dad's."

I stared at her. "How could she?"

"He can be really nice sometimes." Sophie stared off.

"But you'll stay here with us, right?" We both knew I meant *if your mother goes back.*

"But what about my mom?" Sophie started to cry.

I hugged her tight. "I'm here. I'll be your sister forever."

She sniffed. "Yeah. Remember — family business?"

When her mother got home that night, Sophie started in on the silent treatment. I sat with Popcorn and watched "Star Trek" reruns I'd taped on the VCR. It was going to be a rough week and this was only Tuesday.

The next day, I was in the girl's bathroom before gym class when I saw it. I was checking out how much of my eyebrow had grown back in. I could hear the other girls leaving the locker room and heading into the gym. That was when I saw something behind me on the wall. In the mirror, the word was backwards, but it looked familiar. Slowly, I turned around.

There, on the bathroom wall, someone had written my name. Not just once — several times. A lot of other things were written around it: *SLUT, FOR A GOOD TIME CALL JUJUBE GELB,* my phone number. In one corner, different girls had added comments about me, one after the other. It was all the usual stuff, but this time it was about me.

I leaned on the sink and stared at the words. The whole thing felt suddenly ridiculous. This couldn't possibly have anything to do with me. I wanted to laugh, but I couldn't find the place in me that laughed. I felt nothing, as if I was nothing.

I remembered something a guy had said to me in the library that morning. "Hey, Jujube — every time I take a leak, I think about you."

Every time I take a leak. I left my gym stuff in the locker room and walked out into the hall. I knew this was the period Carlos had a spare. He was in the cafeteria, by himself as usual, watching the snow come down.

"I need your help," I said.

"Sure." He followed me down the hall. When I stopped in front of one of the guys' bathrooms, he looked at me, confused.

"I'm going in there," I told him.

Right off, he knew why. "I dunno, Jujube."

"I've got the right to know what they're saying about me."

"You must have the general idea." His eyes were asking me to back off.

I heard my heart thumping as if from a long way off. I just looked at him.

He sighed. "It's your funeral."

Carlos went in to check if anyone was in there. As I waited, I heard the "Star Trek" theme softly in my head. *Go where no woman has gone before,* I thought.

The bathroom was empty. As I went in, Carlos stood guard at the door. I walked along the row of mirrors, in and out of each stall. The worst stuff was written over the urinals. I stood for a long time reading, glad I had my back to Carlos.

When I was finished, when I'd gotten every last word, I turned around. *So this is what they think about me,* I thought. *When they look at me, they think this.*

"Are they all like this — all the guys' cans?" I asked.

Carlos looked alarmed. "You don't want to check them all out, do you?"

"I think I've got the picture," I said.

He blinked quickly, his eyes suddenly red. "If it was one guy, I'd take him on, Jujube. I can't go after everyone."

Neither can I, I thought. "That's never helped anyone before."

"Maybe not." He tried a half grin.

"Thanks."

"Anytime."

When I got home after school, Sophie was watching TV. I sneaked upstairs, dropped down on my bed, and stared up at the ceiling. Popcorn jumped onto the bed and laid his head on my stomach.

Brent's name hadn't been up on any of those walls — just mine. I'd seen the names of other girls. In the back corner of one stall, I'd even found Sophie's name, faded, but still there. I wondered if any of these girls knew their names were up there. I'd never talked to most of them.

But it looked like we had something in common.

The club that doesn't even know it exists, I thought. *Welcome to the Slut Club, Jujube Gelb.*

Chapter Six

The next morning, I decided not to get up. Just for one day, I'd lie in bed and let everything go by. I deserved one day off from hell.

"Hi, Jujube." It was Mom in the doorway.

"Hi, Mom."

"Sophie says you feel sick. What have you got — sore throat? Flu?"

"Sounds good."

As she sat down, I pulled the blankets over my head. I knew she was going to get it all out of me. I wasn't looking forward to it. Mom started to tug at the top of the sheets.

"You seem more heartsick than anything else to me." Her voice was very close. It made me feel like a little kid. Under the blankets, I crawled to the foot of the bed and curled into a ball.

"Hey, where are you going?" Mom asked in surprise.

"I don't want to discuss it," I said through the blankets.

But Mom had followed me down to the end of the bed. She was tugging away, and soon a sliver of light appeared. I grabbed at the blankets. Mom yanked them away. I sat up, blinking after all that dark.

"Honey, what's wrong?" She sat down and put her arms around me. Then she started to stroke my hair. Well, that did me in — knowing how much she wanted me to feel loved. The crying started. When the worst of that was done, the words came out.

"They called me a…" I couldn't say it.

"A what?" Mom asked softly.

It was such a heavy ugly word. I didn't want it in my mouth.

"You can tell me," Mom said.

"A slut," I whispered.

Her arms hugged me tighter. "Say it again," she said.

"Mom!"

"Trust your old mother on this one. I want you to say slut ten times."

I swallowed. She was making this worse.

"C'mon," Mom said.

So I did. At first, I could hardly say it. By the tenth time, I was yelling it. When I was finished, Mom made me say it ten more times. By the end of it, "slut" was coming out of my mouth like any other word.

Mom took my face between her hands. "When you can say a word, you own it. Which means that that word can't do anything to you anymore. It's just a word, Jujube — not your name. Not you."

I blinked and her face came into focus. That was when I noticed she was breathing hard and fast. Usually, this meant someone was in for it.

"I can handle it, Mom. Don't do anything — *please*," I said.

Mom looked ready to tackle the entire football team. "I happen to have a free morning on my hands. I think I'll pay your school a little visit."

"No, Mom!" I scrambled out of bed and followed her out the door. I knew it'd be a bad idea to let her out of my sight.

She looked back over her shoulder. "If you're coming with me, you'd better get dressed."

I got dressed, fast. As soon as she saw me coming down the hall, Mom walked out the front door. "I'll warm up the car while you eat breakfast."

"Mom — " The door shut. *Why'd I have to get a mother who thought it was her job to change the world?* I grabbed my jacket and ran. Mom was driving off before I even got the car door closed.

"This is my problem," I began. One look at her shut me up. She was wearing her Statue of Liberty face, the one she got at her maddest. I think the office secretaries could feel Mom coming. When we walked in, everyone was looking at the door.

"I'd like to speak to the principal of this school," Mom said coldly. "Now."

The nearest secretary began to move. "I'll see if he's free."

"He'd better be," Mom said.

Unfortunately, for the principal, he was free. As we walked into his office, some kids I knew came in for late slips. Their eyes widened when they saw me with my mother. *Wonder how fast this'll hit the bathroom wall?* I wondered.

Mom laid into that principal like the meatpacker she was. She cut and diced him into small pieces, then packed and wrapped him up. When she was done, he'd practically promised to move his office into the nearest guys' bathroom. He looked as if he'd like to suspend some kids for life.

"We don't allow students to write on walls. You must understand it's difficult to catch them at it. To clean it up, we have to hire workmen. Like everyone else, we're short on money right now," he said.

Mom ignored this. "When will it be removed?"

"As soon as possible," the principal said.

Mom gave him a look that seemed to last about a week. "It better be."

But it wasn't. Carlos tried to lie to me.

But I knew from the girls' bathroom that nothing had been done. Maybe all the workmen were on strike, or busy somewhere else. At any rate, now everyone knew my mother had charged in to rescue me.

"Your mom coming on all your dates from now on, Jujube?" became the standard joke.

You've got to be kidding. I'm never going on another date, I thought. I was in the library, watching a girl at the photocopier. I'd seen her name in the guys' bathroom. Finally, I walked over to her.

"Megan?" I asked.

She had on a lot of makeup and a heavy metal T-shirt. "Yeah?"

"I'm Jujube Gelb."

She didn't laugh, didn't look away. "I know."

"You got a minute?" I asked.

"If you got a smoke," she replied.

I didn't, but she came with me

anyway. We found a quiet hall corner by a window and stood looking out. It was hard to get started talking about it. When I did, I found her story was a lot like mine.

"I heard about your mother." She grinned.

I rolled my eyes.

"You're lucky. My parents heard some of the stories and beat the hell out of me. They said they always knew I'd turn out this way."

This way, I thought.

"It can't last forever," I protested.

Megan laughed a little. "Yes, it can. Once they call you a slut, you're a slut."

"You're a person. You're a human being."

"I'm a person who is dying for a smoke," said Megan. She headed off down the hall in search of the nearest pack. I watched her go. There was no way I'd tell Mom anymore about this. Not for the last bit of love in the world.

Chapter Seven

At the end of the week the graffiti was still there. Tired of the porn star looks I was getting, I mostly watched my feet walk around school. That's how I ran right into Carlos on Friday afternoon.

"Walking in your sleep?" he asked.

"I wish."

He stopped laughing. "Ever been in a four-seater plane?"

"No."

"My dad's taking our plane out tomorrow. Want to come?"

"Wow! Sure. Could Sophie come too?" It wasn't that I took Sophie everywhere with me. But with her mother gone this weekend, I knew she could use the lift.

Carlos shrugged. He walked home with me and came in for a bit. Mom fed him cookies and milk while she put him through the third degree. Popcorn laid his head on Carlos's knee with a sigh. I could tell my mother and my dog really liked him. This was important, since he'd be taking me several thousand feet off the ground.

That night, Sophie's mother went over to her father's. Sophie was out too, and didn't get in until 3 a.m. She had her own key, but Mom sleeps with her ear to the ground. In the middle of the night, their voices in the hall woke me up.

"I called your friend's house — you

weren't out with her like you said," Mom said.

"You called her?" Sophie's voice went high.

"It's after three. Anything could've happened to you."

"You don't run my life. I can take care of myself."

"I love you and I want you to be safe."

It got quiet and I lay stiff on my bed. Then Sophie said, "My mom doesn't care about me. Why do you?"

"Your mom cares. You're easy to care about, Sophie. Real easy."

"If my mom loved me, she wouldn't be with that creep. She wouldn't have me all worried and hurting like this!" Sophie yelled.

"You went over there, didn't you?" Mom said.

My mouth fell open and I pulled the pillow over my face. Sophie was going to kill me.

Just like I thought, Sophie said, "Jujube told you?!"

I hung onto my pillow. Then Mom said, "Where else would you be? Your friend's at home. Your boyfriend's at college. Jujube didn't have to tell me."

Their voices went on for a while. I guess Mom calmed her down. When Sophie came into our room, she decided to let me live. All she'd done at her father's place was stand close to the house and listen. She was waiting for the sounds of fighting, but hadn't heard any.

At 8 a.m., I had to beat her awake with my pillow. "Get up, slug."

"Get up?" Sophie groaned. "Why?"

The why showed up an hour later.

Carlos and his father drove up in a car that sounded like it'd lost several mufflers. I wondered if the plane was that bad off. Sophie got into the front seat with

Mr. Rojas. Carlos held the back door open for me. Suddenly, I couldn't move. All I could think was *back seat baby*.

Everyone looked at me, waiting. Then Carlos spoke low, so no one else could hear. "Hey, no hands. Promise."

"Sorry," I muttered, climbing in.

"No prob." He climbed in after me and glued himself to his side of the car. Mr. Rojas started the engine and we blasted out of the driveway.

"Ever been to heaven before?" Carlos yelled, grinning.

Why did this question make me nervous? I shook my head.

"It's O.K. — you get to come back," he said.

It was a warm March day, the snow almost gone. We stood on the tarmac, the breeze blowing the hair back from our faces. Carlos wore his jean jacket and a T-shirt as usual. His grin came and went like quick thoughts, and his eyes seemed darker. He had Sophie laughing, forgetting about her mother. Then we saw Mr. Rojas taxi the plane toward us, the sun running off the wings. Something in Carlos seemed to almost lift him off the ground.

This guy is gorgeous, I thought.

Mr. Rojas opened the passenger door. "Jujube — you get into the front seat with me."

Carlos's face went blank. Sophie punched him in the shoulder and said, "Stuck with me."

It sure is noisy in a small plane. We began to taxi down the runway, the world going by more and more quickly. Then the plane lifted a little, rocked softly in the air, rose a little again. Trees were dropping away, the sky coming down to meet us. Down below, the city shrank to a toy town — there was downtown, the river, and my school. How could such a tiny place hold so much trouble?

We were out of the city now, over brown fields with patches of snow. Mr. Rojas asked me, "Want to try the wheel?"

From the back seat came loud shrieks. Carlos shouted, "No, Dad, no!"

"Let me out of here!" howled Sophie.

The two of them went on dying with terror. Mr. Rojas grinned and pointed to a dial on the dashboard. "Keep your eyes on this. It tells you if you're keeping the plane level."

There were two steering wheels, one in front of me. I put both hands on mine.

"Dad — I haven't written my will yet," Carlos yelled.

So much for moral support. Mr. Rojas flipped the switch and I was flying the plane. I couldn't believe it — it felt like I had the sky in my hands. Mr. Rojas pointed out the window. "That's good, Jujube. Over there you can see Leduc."

I had a cousin who lived in Leduc. I

looked for her house, but then the streets seemed to be getting bigger. I heard Mr. Rojas gasp. He grabbed his wheel and we came up out of a nosedive.

"Oops," I said.

"Oops?!" screeched Sophie.

"We warned you, Dad," Carlos said.

"Can I try again?" I asked.

"Maybe in a little while," Mr. Rojas mumbled. He looked pale, so I decided not to bug him about it. One heart attack per day is enough for an adult. Kids handle five to ten, but you've got to go easy on adults.

We flew around for over an hour. Coming back, I saw our school again, underneath us. I took a deep breath and felt very light. *It's that school that's the problem, not me,* I thought. I wasn't going to let it drag me down again.

Back on the ground, Sophie, Carlos, and I watched the plane taxi to the hangar. "O.K.?" asked Carlos. He was so close, but not touching me. We stood looking at each other. Beside us, Sophie coughed.

"You started that project for English yet?" I asked him.

He shrugged. "Not till the night before it's due."

"Want to work on it with me?"

"Sure. Got a topic?"

"I want to do it on graffiti," I said.

"Wow," Sophie said.

One eyebrow went up, but Carlos looked interested. "Any graffiti in particular?" he asked.

I laughed. "Very particular."

He nodded. "How're you going to get Old Dead Lips to go for it?"

"It's supposed to be about ways we communicate," I said. "Ways we pass ideas back and forth. The graffiti on that bathroom wall is sure passing ideas around about me. And I've got some ideas about that."

"I bet you do," Sophie grinned.

"Maybe I've got some too," Carlos said.

Chapter Eight

Monday, Carlos and I took our cameras to school. I skipped gym again so we could work at the same time. He covered the guys' bathrooms and I covered the girls'. Most of them were empty because classes were on. I stood at the first wall, the camera in my hand.

The wall was old. I could see it needed repairs. The words looked as if they'd been there forever, almost a part of the brick itself. *SLUT* was the first word I took a picture of. *JUJUBE GELB IS A SLUT.* I focused carefully. The shutter whirred and clicked.

As I walked around those walls snapping pictures, something happened. It was as if, somewhere, I was stepping over an invisible line. As if I was finally saying to everyone, "You can't make me take this anymore." As if I had my life back and was I ever going to make it move.

For several days, Carlos and I went around downtown and the malls, snapping pictures of graffiti. Carlos had even gotten a shot of a guy writing on a bathroom wall.

"Who's that?" I asked.

"He's in grade twelve. I don't know his name," Carlos said.

"Well, he knows mine," I said. He was adding to a list of comments about my nightlife.

"He doesn't know you," Carlos said.

A warm feeling came and went in me, like a breath.

"You're a good guy, y'know that, Carlos?"

Carlos went a little red. It seemed to take him a while to breathe again. I wanted to touch him. But I didn't. Then he shrugged.

"I got a lot of hassle when my family first came to Canada. It was because I couldn't speak English. I flunked grade three. The kids made fun of me, called me names. Most of the first English words I learned were the names they called me. I remember thinking English words were not friendly. So I guess I know what it can be like."

After we got the prints developed, we sat down with Sophie. She was in grade twelve, so she knew the older girls. Between us, we figured out who owned the names on those walls. Then I went around school, tracking the girls down. Some were pretty embarrassed. But most agreed to come to a meeting.

We held it in a back corner of the cafeteria at lunchtime. Sophie, Carlos, and I waited. Slowly, the table filled up with girls — maybe fifteen or so. Some looked tough, some were popular. There was one nerd. I could see other kids starting to watch us. There were guys out there who kept looking at us, then away, back again, away. *There's only one way they could know why we were all together,* I thought.

When it looked like everyone had arrived, I put down my sandwich. I said, "Welcome to the first meeting of the Slut Club."

Some of the girls jerked. Megan, the girl I'd talked to before, started to laugh.

"I don't think it's funny," said a popular girl.

"Neither do I," I said.

"Well, then why say it?" she asked.

"Because I'm not going to let that word bother me anymore. It belongs on a bathroom wall, not in my gut," I explained.

"Yeah, I guess you're right," she said.

"The school says they can't clean up the walls right now. They don't have the money," I told them.

"Yeah, right." Megan rolled her eyes.

"That doesn't mean *we* can't do anything. Carlos and I are doing an English project on graffiti. We took pictures of the bathroom walls. We want your permission to show them."

I passed the pictures around. As the girls looked at them, I watched their faces, the hurt in them. I let them look until they were finished and their eyes were back on me. I said, "In a way, I'm glad the school doesn't have the money right now. Painting over those words would be like a Band-Aid — just covering it all up. You don't change things by covering them up."

"Yeah," someone nodded.

"We'd like to use these pictures in our English project. But your names belong to you. We won't use them if you don't want us to," I said.

"What're you going to do?" Megan asked.

So I told them, with Carlos throwing in a few words. Some of the girls began to nod, some even smiled. Several backed out and left the meeting, but a couple offered to help. After we'd finished figuring it all out, Sophie took down everyone's phone number. Carlos collected the pictures again.

Megan leaned across the table. Definitely loud enough for Carlos to hear, she grinned and asked, "Is he yours?"

Sophie giggled. I figured I was about as red as a human being could get. There was no way I was looking at Carlos to see how he was taking this.

Megan grinned again. "Oops —

sorry I asked."

I looked at my hands and said, "He's his."

Then I glanced at him just as he looked at me. Our eyes bumped into each other and hung on.

"Ahhhh — they're in love," Megan sighed.

"Give us a break," Carlos groaned.

"This meeting is over now. Please," I added.

Chapter Nine

All weekend, Carlos and I worked at my house. We had to get our English project together for Monday. All weekend, we watched Sophie's mother pack and leave. She was moving back in with her husband. Sophie was going to stay with us — Mom had made that very clear.

"You are my second daughter, Sophie," Mom told her. Mom can be very dramatic, but it's great when she likes you.

Sophie didn't talk to her mother all weekend. She didn't help her pack. Arms around her legs, Sophie sat very still in front of the TV. Whenever I heard the "Star Trek" theme, I knew where Sophie was going — far, far away. Late Sunday afternoon, her mother dragged the last of her stuff to the front door. That was when Sophie finally moved from the TV. Her head came around and she stared at her mother. Then she gave a cry like a little kid.

"Mom!"

She jumped up and ran to her mother, throwing out her arms. Their bodies went tight around each other and they hugged for a long time. Then Sophie let her mother go and watched her walk to the car.

"I didn't think she'd really do it," she said softly.

I stood beside her in the doorway. "Maybe she'll come back."

"She thinks all the bad stuff with Dad is over now. All gone — just like that." Sophie snapped her fingers.

"Too bad," I whispered.

"He won't go see a counselor. He won't say he has a problem. They're just going to pretend none of it happened, but I know he'll do it again." Sophie looked straight at me. "Like I pretended those rumors about me weren't going around at school. Y'know, even if they went in now and painted those bathroom walls, the stories would still be going around. You're doing the right thing with that project, Jujube."

"Thanks," I said. I sure hoped she was right.

Monday morning felt like a decision a long time in the making. English was our first class. As the other kids came in, Carlos and I set up the screen and the slide projector. I didn't look at Brent, but the whole time I knew where he was. Old Dead Lips sat down at the back.

Carlos ran the slide projector. I stood beside the screen talking about different kinds of graffiti. The lights were off and I couldn't see much of anyone. First we showed graffiti from the railway tunnels and the bridges, downtown. There was laughter, whispers when kids saw something they recognized. The area around Brent kept pretty quiet. Old Dead Lips sat without comment, letting the dirty words go by.

I knew when the high school ones were coming up. Carlos set the projector on high speed. Then he sat, both hands folded on his desk like he was praying for me. I waited for the names of the other girls to finish. Then I stepped in front of the screen. The words hit me full force.

SLUT, it said across my chest. *JUJUBE GELB IS A SLUT.*

There were gasps from the kids as word after word flashed over me. Old Dead Lips started to stand, then sat down slowly. After a while, there was silence and the steady clicking of the projector.

A different kind of sex ed class, I thought to myself.

"You'd think words were the easiest thing in the world to give and take," I told them all. "They're free, easy to come by. They don't get taxed. Anyone can own a word, use it any way she likes."

The bathroom wall kept up its steady flashing over my face. "What's in a word? You can't eat a word, drink a word, build it or take it down. You can't touch a word, but a word can touch you. Like 'slut.'" In spite of Mom, the word still felt heavy, dirty in my mouth. I paused.

"Lately, it's been harder than usual to get out of bed in the morning. There's such a long day ahead. I have so many decisions to make. If I wear this shirt, the collar doesn't go up to my chin. So will I look like a slut if I wear it? If I put on these jeans, will someone think they're tight like a slut's? They'll be sure to let me know.

"I watch the way I walk down the halls. I think, Do I walk like a slut? Do I stand at my locker like a slut? The look in my eye — do I look at people like a slut? Do I breathe like a slut? *Am I a slut?*"

I took a deep breath. The room seemed to be short on air. "Everyone knows a slut isn't really a human being. She's something you kick around and take dirty pictures of. You can laugh, say anything you want about her because she's not like you anymore. Maybe she used to be. Maybe she used to be a normal, regular kid. But then someone called her a slut and turned her into a thing. A *nothing*.

"So the word slut goes up on the bathroom wall about me. How do I argue with a word like that? Once it's up there, it's case closed. Nothing left to decide. It's just a word, but it still takes away my choices — what I can wear, how I can walk, even how I think about myself."

I said it again. *"Slut.* That word could run my life . . . *if I believed it."*

No one else said a word. The slides had ended. I stood in the white light on the screen, free of their words. As we packed up, kids came over to Carlos and me. They didn't say much. Some touched our shoulders or nodded. Old Dead Lips told us he'd given us an A. He cracked a one-inch smile, then said, "Words cannot express how I feel."

Out in the hall after class, we saw the Slut Club had been busy. We'd all made a lot of posters out of the bathroom wall graffiti. During the last class, Sophie and the others had put them up in the school halls. Now, kids crowded around them, their mouths like very large holes. It wasn't the words themselves that were the shock. It was the place they were written. Next to a toilet, they fit right in. Out in the school hallway, they didn't.

Mom's right, I thought. *It's not the words. It's the way they're used.*

Brent Floyd was nowhere to be seen. I imagined the principal running through the halls, tearing the pictures down at warp speed.

"He can't take much more of this, Captain. His engine will blow for sure," I muttered.

"Huh?" asked Carlos.

"Nothing," I grinned.

Chapter Ten

When Carlos and I walked into the house after school, we could hear Mom and Sophie talking. Popcorn lay in the hallway, whining.

"C'mon, I'm hungry," said Sophie. She was in Mom's bedroom.

Mom sounded firm. "You've had enough."

Oh no, Sophie's at it again, I thought.

We saw Mom standing in front of her bed, holding a box of graham crackers. Sophie was facing her. Suddenly, Sophie burst into giggles, ran at Mom, and toppled her onto the bed. A tickle fight developed.

I rolled my eyes at Carlos. "This is what I live with."

Pinned on the bed, Sophie noticed us. She howled, "Go get me some food! There's nothing to eat in the house. I'm starving to death!"

"Did you give your project?" Mom got up and came toward the door. Right away, Sophie went for the graham crackers.

"Jujube was great," Carlos said.

"Of course she was." Mom grabbed at the graham crackers. Everything was pretty much back to normal — even my eyebrow had grown in again. There was only one last thing to take care of.

By the end of the week, the school found the money to paint over the graffiti. The Slut Club decided to have a party to celebrate. One of the girls bought a cake and twelve candles — one for each of us. We sat in a back hall, singing "Happy birthday to clean walls!" After eating the cake we joked about Carlos. Then everyone started in on Carlos and me. O.K., O.K. — so it was official. We were going out.

"Ahhhh — they're in love," Megan sighed.

"Shut up," Sophie told her, laughing.

Megan turned up her radio and we tossed a hackeysack back and forth. I heard a door close farther down the hall and looked up from the game. A guy was coming toward us, his head down. He hadn't seen me yet or he wouldn't have kept coming. It was Brent.

The other girls noticed me staring and fell quiet. The radio kept blasting as the twelve of us watched him walk toward us. I couldn't believe that he didn't even look up. When he was just about ready to walk through the middle of us, Megan cut her radio. He looked up, saw me, saw all of us watching him, and stopped dead.

He's scared, I thought.

Sophie gave a puppy growl and said, "Woof, woof."

Brent flushed and the girls laughed.

"Jujube." Brent's voice cracked.

Carlos stiffened.

"Yeah?" I gave Brent a dead fish glare. His face was red now — a definite red. He took a deep breath.

"Y'know, *none* of this came from me. I swear, I didn't say a word about you."

I just looked at him. My hands were in fists again.

"It was the other guys." Brent was talking quickly, his eyes darting everywhere. "They asked why we were out at my car. They started joking about it, then everyone started in on it."

"Yeah, I remember," I said.

Suddenly, Carlos asked, "When the other guys started joking around, what did you say?"

"Nothing," Brent insisted.

"Let me get this straight. They started telling crude jokes about me and you said *nothing?!*" I demanded.

I could see it happening. The other guys asked the questions, made the jokes. Brent sat there silent with a smirk on his face.

Brent took a few steps back. "Hey, it was just a joke. Why'd you have to take it so personally?"

"For you, it was a joke. For me, it was my life," I said.

"Yeah, I guess. Like I said — sorry." Brent turned and walked away.

For a second, none of us moved. Then Sophie wound up and fired the hackeysack. Her aim was perfect. She hit

Brent right in the butt. He broke into a jog
and ducked out a side door.

I grinned. "I think the Slut Club
should have regular meetings — keep this
school in line."

Carlos bumped my shoulder with his.
"Keep the world in line?"

I looked at his lips. They were so
close. I could spend a lot of time kissing
them. "Maybe. But then, maybe I'm too
busy," I said.

"Ahhh," Megan sighed.

orca soundings

Orca Soundings is a new teen fiction series that features realistic teenage characters in stories that focus on contemporary situations and problems.

Soundings are short, thematic novels ideal for class or independent reading. Written by such stalwart teen authors as William Bell and Beth Goobie, there will be between eight and ten new titles a year.

For more information please call Orca Book Publishers at 1-800-210-5277.

Other titles in the Orca Soundings series: